Walk With Me

Meditations
on the Way of the Cross

DEVISED BY
GERALD COATES

MCCRIMMONS
Great Wakering   Essex

First published in Great Britain in 1994 by
McCRIMMON PUBLISHING CO. LTD.
10-12 High Street, Great Wakering, Essex SS3 0EQ.
Telephone: (0702) 218956   Fax: (0702) 216082

Devised by
GERALD COATES, Church of Christ the King, Steyning.

Woodcarvings
CHRIS SHAWCROSS

Text
CHRIS MCDONNELL
Scriptural quotations taken from Jerusalem Bible, published and copyright
1966, 1967 and 1968 by Darton, Longman and Todd Ltd and Doubleday &
Co. Inc, and used by permission of the publishers.

ISBN 0 85597 531 8

Design and layout by Nick Snode
Typeset in 12 & 11 pt Palatino by McCrimmons
Edited by Sue Simpson
Colour reproduction by Genesis Image Data Processing, London
Printed on Sequel 115gsm
Printed by Black Bear Press Ltd, Cambridge

Foreword

HEAVENLY FATHER

YOUR SON has trodden the path before us
May we draw strength to go forward
knowing that today we will have to face
nothing that will be like HIS SUFFERING.

Whatever we may have to face
HIS STRENGTH and POWER
will keep us firmly on the path
YOU have mapped out for us.
For this we thank YOU through
that same JESUS CHRIST OUR LORD.

AMEN

Gerald Coates

In the name of the Father,
the Son,
and the Holy Spirit.

We sign ourselves
with the Cross of Christ.

Father,
in Baptism we were signed
with the Cross of Christ.

There is an urgency
in our Christian lives
that allows no pause
for we are indeed
a pilgrim people.

We cannot stand still
we cannot remain the same.

As now we meditate again
on the Way of the Cross
we continue on our journey,
seeking yourself.

Be with us Lord
as we accept the Cross
that each of us must carry.

Jesus is condemned to death

The High Priest put a second question to him.
'Are you the Christ, the Son of the Blessed One?'
'I am', said Jesus.

MARK 61: 14

The Prisoner,
looking beyond his captors,
said little in his own defence,
responding only in honesty and truth.

Because of this,
they had already agreed his guilt.

Lord,
we hear your voice
declaring

(for all who will listen)

the mystery of Incarnation.

We seek your silent face
and acknowledge our need
for forgiveness.

Jesus carries his Cross

*And when they had finished making fun of him,
they took off the cloak and dressed him in his own
clothes, and led him away to crucify him.*

MATTHEW 31: 27

Condemned,
He was taken
by force of arms
at dawn.

Having beaten him,
they led him away
for execution
to a place
beyond the city limits.

Lord,
you accepted your Cross
and began your final journey;
- it had to be done.

May I accept my Cross,
understanding that
my journey
cannot be made without it.

The First Fall

Meanwhile, Peter was sitting outside in the courtyard and a servant girl came up to him and said: 'You were with Jesus the Galilean'.
But he denied it.   MATTHEW 69-70: 26

Weakened,
his footsteps faltered
as he stumbled,
hand outstretched,
fearful of the ground.

His friend watched the Galilean fall,
and said - nothing.

Lord,
our lack of faith
breaks the rhythm of our footfall
and the closing earth
surrounds us.

There is darkness
loneliness
and emptiness
as we ask

'Where are you?'

A mother meets her son

At Cana, in Galilee, Jesus had said, 'Woman, why turn to me? My time has not come yet'. His Mother said to the servants 'Do whatever he tells you.'

JOHN 4-5: 2

Prevented
by the force of arms
from coming close,
a Mother seeks her Son.

The disappeared one
taken from her in the night.

Soon she will be left
with only her memories.

Lord,
how can a Mother see
her Son suffer
and not suffer herself?

Yet, step by step,
she stayed with you,
from a Stable to Nazareth
and on to Cana.

In a short while,
she will be found
standing
by the Cross.

Now,
in this press
of Passover people,
she is with you.

Walk with me,
Mary,
on the path I must travel.
Stay with me.

Simon helps to carry the Cross

As they were leading him away, they seized on a man, Simon, from Cyrene, who was coming in from the country and made him shoulder the Cross and carry it behind Jesus.

LUKE 26: 23

Unable
to walk on alone,
a man taken from the crowd
is told to help him.

There is no choice.

Condemned men must die
- at the appropriate place -
for the sake of the people.

Lord,
Simon was a face
from the crowd,
an extra shoulder
and a pair of hands
to share the load.

May we give to others
a lift on the way,

expecting nothing,
offering everything.

His face is wiped by Veronica

*Large numbers of people followed him, and of women,
too, who mourned and lamented for him.*

LUKE 27: 23

Sweating
with exhaustion
from his ill treatment,
he pauses for breath.

A woman,
ignoring personal risk,
wipes his face with a cloth.

Her kindness done,
she becomes again
another person,
one among many,
- street side faces
on a Friday morning.

Lord,
who she was,
where she came from,
does not matter.

She cared enough
to risk all
- and asked nothing in return.

The Second Fall

When he went out to the gateway, another servant girl saw him and said to the people there: 'This man was with Jesus the Nazarene.' And again with an oath he denied it.

MATTHEW 72: 27

Broken
by pain,
he falls again.

The Nazarene,
eyesight blurred,
momentarily sees his friend
gazing at him.

But neither can speak.
He turns and is gone.

Lord,
Peter was a fearful man
and he acted out of fear.

His denial was our denial,
day after day,
year after year.

Sometimes we, too, claim
that we do not know you,
fearful of the cost.

Maybe tomorrow Lord,
maybe it will be easier then.

The Jerusalem women meet him

Jesus turned to the women and said: 'Daughters of Jerusalem, do not weep for me: weep rather for yourselves and your children.'

LUKE 28: 23

Protesting
at his treatment
by the authorities,
the Women of Peace
gather by the road.

A passing word,
and they move him on.

The women are left
weeping,
confused.

Lord,
too often
women have raised their voices
at the folly of men.

Too often
they have been ignored.

May we, their children,
listen to their words
and their cries;

and hearing them,
hear you.

The Third Fall

A little later, the bystanders came up and said to Peter, 'You are one of them for sure! Why your accent gives you away.' Then he started calling down curses on himself and swearing 'I do not know the man.'

MATTHEW 73-74: 26

Beaten,
but now within sight of the Hill,
face down in the dust.
Unrecognisable.

Voiceless.

'Get up, we've a job to do.'

Lord,
time and again
we almost make it,
and turning,
dejected and disheartened,
we realise our failure.

Even then, Lord,
you are with us.

It's time
we were moving,

It's time
to start again.

Jesus is stripped

*I can count every one of my bones
and there they glare at me, gloating.*   PSALM 22: 17-18

*They shared out my clothing among them
They cast lots for my clothes.*   JOHN 24: 19

Stripped,
he is prepared
for public shame.

Bruised, he is silent.

With shoulders bared
he accepts the inevitable.

Besides,
the crowd are waiting.

Lord,
strip me
of all I carry;

strip me
of everything
that prevents me from
carrying my Cross.

And when
I am stripped
be there
to sustain me.

Jesus is nailed to the Cross

When they reached the place called the Skull,
they crucified him there.

LUKE 33: 23

Nailed
to the wooden frame
that stretched wide his arms
and secured his feet,
there, on the Hill,
he is raised above the people.

Lord,
the hammering of nails
has echoed across this earth
as we repeatedly crucify you.

Man against man,
nation against nation.

Yet
from that Cross of Suffering
with failing voice you called,

'Father forgive them
for they do not know what they do.'

Father, forgive us.

Jesus dies on the Cross

It was now about the sixth hour and with the sun eclipsed,
a darkness came over the whole land until the ninth hour.
The veil of the temple was torn right down the middle and
when Jesus had cried out in a loud voice, he said 'Father into
your hands I commend my spirit'.
With these words he breathed his last.   LUKE 44-46: 23

Naked
on the Cross,
he gazed at those whose fists
were raised in anger,
until he could see no more.

There, in the late afternoon,
with head bowed,
body and spirit exhausted,
he ceased the struggle. It was done.

Lord,
how are we to understand
those hours late on a Friday
before Passover?

How can we share the emptiness
of those who walked with you,
seeing you now defeated,
hung between thieves?

So this was where all the
hours and days of
walking and talking
finally ended.

Defeat on a Hill - and a satisfied crowd - Finished.

Jesus is taken down from the Cross

Take care of every bone
Yahweh will not let one be broken.

PSALM 34: 20

Lifeless,
his savaged body
lay, once again,
in the caring arms
of his Mother.

Journey over.
Task complete.

Failure in the sight of men.

Lord,
the final act
of your friends
was to accept
your lifeless body
for burial.

Accept, Lord,
our failures,
our mistakes
and our careless ways.

Bury them, Lord,
with the suffering of your Cross.

The burial of Jesus

They took the body of Jesus and wrapped it with spices in linen cloths, following the custom of Jewish burial.
JOHN 40: 19

Burial
did not take long.

Laying him out nearby
(before the last light
   and the coming Festival)
covering him with a cloth.

'It is time we were gone.'

Turning into the dusk
they left him.

Lord,
it is over,
the Way of the Cross
has been walked.

The story has been told
and prophecy fulfilled.

'What now?'

they must have said to one another
as they walked into the chill night air.

Resurrection

*Jesus said 'Mary.' She knew him then and said
to him in Hebrew 'Rabboni!'*

JOHN 16: 20

Morning
and first light in the garden,
brings shadows of women moving.

Turning,
they did not recognise
in this Springtime Pasch,
the Nazarene
passing over into Galilee.

Contained in the finger space
of the morning dawn,
the Resurrected Christ
greets us.

Rabboni,
we did not trust you,
we did not understand.

We thought it was over.

'No, my people,
it has just begun.'

Father,
we have shared again
the Passover journey
of your Son.

We have followed
his Way of the Cross.

As Christian people
we understand
that must be our way too.

Help us through this
Prayer of the Cross
to seek your will for us.

We sign ourselves
with the Cross of Christ

In the name of the Father
the Son,
and the Holy Spirit.

Afterword

As we make the Way of the Cross with Jesus today
may His Passion become our way too.

Each of us has to carry the Cross of Life.
May each Station place us firmly on the path
to our Resurrection.

Life is a journey and we look back
to assure ourselves we are going in
the right direction.

Keep us firmly on the true path, not
flinching from any suffering
this may entail
and when we tend to falter
may we always remember
the joy of the life to come.

Gerald Coates

A brief historical note

The Stations of the Cross are a series of pictures or images representing the different incidents in the last journey of Christ from Pilate's house to the entombment.

Usually they are ranged around the church with the first Station on one side of the High Altar, and the last on the other. Sometimes they are erected in the open along a road to a church, or up a hill to a shrine.

The devotion probably grew up out of the practice of pilgrims visiting Jerusalem, who from an early date had followed the traditional route from Pilate's house to Calvary, and on returning home, had wished to reproduce the devotion in their own churches. They are intended to help us make a pilgrimage in spirit to the scene of Christ's suffering and death.

The devotion was developed by the Franciscans who were the guardians of the holy places in Jerusalem. It is a popular devotion, especially during Lent and Passiontide, to visit the Stations in order, reciting a prayer and meditating at each incident.

The number of Stations has varied at different times and from place to place, sometimes being as few as six. The present number of fourteen was not finally established until the nineteenth century.
The Resurrection (as the fifteenth Station) is a twentieth century addition.

The Stations at Steyning

The Stations have been donated by individuals and groups within the parish in memory of their deceased relatives, with three exceptions. The first Station is in celebration and thanksgiving for Fr. MacHale's ministry as first Parish Priest in Steyning. The second Station is dedicated to the people of Ireland.
The fifteenth Station is for the Parishioners.

The Stations begin on the right hand side of the altar, and go clockwise round the church ending with the Resurrection.

The woods were carefully chosen to blend in with the existing wooden features in the church. The base of each Station is Oak, the figures are Lime and the crosses Paddux, a deep reddish-purple wood.

The new Stations were dedicated on 26th March 1993.

Matching posters and slides are also available.